The Rourke Guide
to State Symbols

LICENSE PLATES

Tracy Maurer

The Rourke Press, Inc.
Vero Beach, Florida 32964

PHOTO CREDITS:
East Coast Studios would like to thank Mike Sells for loaning images from his extensive U.S. plates collection. Also thanks to Michael Kustemann for use of some great plate images from his collection

COVER ILLUSTRATION: Jim Spence

CREATIVE SERVICES:
East Coast Studios, Merritt Island, Florida

EDITORIAL SERVICES:
Janice L. Smith for Penworthy

Library of Congress Cataloging-in-Publication Data

Maurer, Tracy, 1965-
    License plates / Tracy Maurer.
        p. cm. — (The Rourke guide to state symbols)
    Includes index.
    ISBN 1-57103-298-3
    1. Automobile license plates—United States. 2. Signs and symbols—United States.   I. Title. II. Series.
HE5620.L5M35 1999
929.9—dc21   99-32996
                                                                                CIP

Printed in the USA

TABLE OF CONTENTS

INTRODUCTION

Since the early 1900s, each state has issued its own license plates or "tags." These metal plates identify the vehicle and its owner. Many license plates feature state symbols. They may also have state nicknames on them. Often, the plate designs look very pretty. Thousands of people collect license plates as a hobby.

License plates begin as blank metal sheets. A machine stamps the letters and numbers into the metal. Then colored ink is rolled over the raised parts. Reflective plates have a special coating made of millions of tiny glass beads. This coating helps the plates look brighter in the dark than plates with normal ink.

The numbers and letters on license plates often use codes to show where the vehicle's home county is, when the registration expires, and other useful data. Vehicle owners belonging to certain groups may receive plates with special designs or symbols on them. For example, disabled persons have wheelchair symbols on their plates.

Each state issues more than twelve different plates and uses its own codes. Many Native American tribes also issue plates. Plates change over time as well, so hundreds of different plates exist. You will find only a sample included in this book. When you're riding in the car, watch for all the different plates going by!

ALABAMA

"Heart of Dixie"

1945

1983

1998

University of Alabama

In 1912, Alabama released its first state-issued license plate. Designs have changed many times over the years. Since 1955, Alabama has featured a heart on its plate to match its nickname. Vehicle owners today can choose the standard plate with its fancy script and star-filled sky or special-issue plates. Special-issue plates let the vehicle owner show support for an Alabama college, the environment, education, the arts or other interests.

ALASKA

"The Last Frontier"

1966

1976

1998

University of Alaska

Alaska's license plates, first issued in 1921, featured the state flag. A totem pole graced the plates in 1966 and 1967. A grizzly bear and mountain scene appeared in 1976 and ran for about six years. The state issued a special Centennial Alaska Gold Rush plate in 1998 only. Many people traded in their blue-on-gold "Last Frontier" plates for these beautiful and highly collectible ones.

ARIZONA

"Grand Canyon State"

1934

1969

1995

1998

Arizona first issued state plates in 1914. Three years later, the state placed a steer head on its plates—the first picture on a U.S. license plate. In 1934 Arizona became the first state to stamp a patent number on the plate edge. Beginning in 1940, the "Grand Canyon State" nickname appeared on Arizona plates. Today's license plate shows a colorful desert scene with a cactus and the state nickname.

ARKANSAS
"The Natural State"

1945

1960

1962

1998

The first state-issued license plates in Arkansas were offered in 1911. Through 1913, these were porcelain plates. Many different slogans have been used since then. In 1935, "Centennial Celebration 36" honored the state's beginning. "Opportunity Land" appeared in 1941. The state used "Land of Opportunity" in 1950 and introduced "The Natural State" in 1989. On regular plates, the nickname and state name are blue on white.

CALIFORNIA
"The Golden State"

1919

1945

1984

1998

Five different passenger vehicle license plates are valid in California today. Some plates issued from 1963 to 1986 have gold ink on dark blue. The order of the letters and numbers switched in 1970. A sunburst style appeared in 1987, followed by a nearly plain white plate in 1988. The most current plate has red script letters on white. Colorful special-issue plates add to the variety of California license plates.

COLORADO

"Centennial State"

1933

1958

1970s

1998

Colorado first issued license plates in 1913. Collectors look for the porcelain versions issued through 1915. The 1958 plate featured a skier with the slogan "Colorful" on it. Collectors especially look for the reflective skier plates from Summit County starting with the number 66. Today's plates feature white ink on green mountains. Vehicle owners can also pay extra for more colorful designer plates.

CONNECTICUT
"Constitution State"

1952

1976—Truck

1976—Dealer

1998

Connecticut's colonists wrote a constitution in the 1630s, believed to be the world's first. The "Constitution State" nickname has appeared on car plates since 1974. Current plates, issued in pairs for the vehicle's front and rear, feature the nickname on the bottom and a small white state shape in the upper left corner. Older plates do not have the state shape and the nickname is at the top. The state requires only the rear plate for the older style.

DELAWARE
"The First State"

1941

1943

1963 (with '76 tab)

1997

Unlike other license plates, Delaware plates are flat. A special process prints the gold letters and numbers onto the blue metal instead of stamping them. Delaware's regular plates use only numbers, but letters precede the numbers on special types of vehicles. For example, "A" means ambulance, while "T" means trailer. Delaware issues more than twenty of these lettered plates, plus many choices of special picture plates.

FLORIDA

"The Sunshine State"

1926

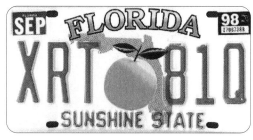

1998

Challenger

Environmental

Known as the "Sunshine State" since 1949, Florida now lets each county decide whether to stamp the county name or the state nickname on license plates. Most counties stamp their names into the plates. The state name and a green state map beneath a picture of an orange complete the design. Special license plates have helped raise money for causes such as saving the manatee and supporting the Special Olympics.

GEORGIA

"Peach State"

1941

1958

1998

Olympics

Georgia switched to a new reflective license plate design in 1997. It features the slogan "Georgia...On My Mind," which is also the official state song. A large peach adds color to the center of the plate. The new design appears on almost all passenger car license plates, but vehicle owners may also choose from special-issue license plates. Designs that support certain colleges and universities are very popular.

HAWAII

"Aloha State"

1942

1976

1998

"Aloha," the famous Hawaiian greeting, has appeared on license plates since the state first issued plates in 1959. A colorful rainbow arches over the slogan on a white field to make today's Hawaiian plates a favorite of many collectors. The simple reflective design helps the license plates show up more clearly at night, too. The letter code used on the license plates tells police from which of Hawaii's four counties the vehicle comes.

IDAHO

"The Gem State"

1928

1985

2000

Idaho began issuing license plates in 1913 and has used seven different slogans since then. Current plates combine both "Scenic" and "Famous Potatoes" sayings on a red, white and blue picture of trees and mountains. Vehicle owners may choose one of two colorful designs supporting conservation instead of the standard plates. Idaho also issues special plates for the state police, veterans, legislators, street rod owners, and National Guard members.

ILLINOIS
"Land of Lincoln"

1927

1956

1998

1998

Illinois issues more types of plates than any other state. Most of these plates are for non-passenger vehicles, such as buses, farm machinery, taxis or big trucks. The state also issues more than 100 different plates for special events, such as parades. These are valid for just 60 days. The standard plate shows the state name and nickname in a blue banner on top of a white base. Vehicle owners may also opt for special designer plates.

INDIANA

"The Crossroads of America"

1945

1978

1999

Five interstate highways meet in Indianapolis, the capital of Indiana. This has earned the city and state the nickname "Crossroads of America." The newest plates use this nickname and a yellow state map with shooting stars on a white base. The first two numbers, up to 99, show the vehicle's home county. Vehicle owners may choose special plates supporting the environment, education and the Children's Trust instead of the standard plates.

IOWA

"The Hawkeye State"

1929

1997

"Kids" Plate

Iowa takes great pride in its farming heritage and modern cities. To honor both, the new license plates show a farm scene below a city skyline. A sticker shows the home county, unlike the former plates that used embossed, or stamped, county names. Fans of the Cyclones, Hawkeyes or Panther university teams may pay extra for special team plates. A special environmental plate is also available.

KANSAS

"Sunflower State"

1941

1957

1990

1997

Kansas first issued license plates in 1913. Collectors especially look for the 1951 to 1955 plates cut into the shape of the state. Each of these plates had a "missing corner" where the Missouri River forms the northeastern side of the state. Although its nickname is the "Sunflower State," Kansas ranks as one of the country's leading sources of wheat. Today's standard plates show shafts of wheat on a yellow and blue base.

KENTUCKY

"Bluegrass State"

1944

1953

1998

1999

Green rolling hills form the base of the newest Kentucky plates. A blue sky with one large cloud tops the scene. But it's not just any cloud—it's in the shape of the state! Since 1988, Kentucky has used its nickname on most license plates. It appears below the state name on the current design. For an additional fee, motorists in Kentucky may choose a blue or yellow environmental plate or a college plate instead of the standard design.

LOUISIANA

"The Bayou State"

1937

1958

1998

University of New Orleans

Louisiana began issuing license plates in 1915 and has used the "Sportsman's Paradise" slogan more than any other over the years. The words appear in blue block letters at the bottom of the newest design. The state name, flowing in a red script style, floats at the top of the white plate. Louisiana offers many special plates as well as this standard design, including plates for the hearing impaired, veterans and firefighters.

20

MAINE

"Vacationland"

1917

1987

Environmental

In 1987, Maine became the first state to show a crustacean, a lobster, on its plates. This image of the famous red sea creature is also one of the few pictures of food on license plates. The motto "Vacationland" appears beneath the lobster. Maine has used this caption on license plates since 1936. The state has created many different designs for special groups, too, such as legislators, veterans or city vehicle operators.

MARYLAND

"Old Line State"

1927

1992

Environmental

A reflective white base and black letters show off the colorful state shield on Maryland's current plates. For an extra fee, vehicle owners may switch to a fund-raising plate for the Chesapeake Bay. Certain group members may also choose from more than 70 different specialty plates. These plates use a group letter code. For example, "EAA" might precede the numbers. The caption, "Experimental Aircraft Association," explains the code.

MASSACHUSETTS

"Bay State"

1915

1977

1995

Environmental

"The Spirit of America" license plates with their red, white and blue design first appeared in 1987 as specialty plates. In 1993, Massachusetts began using the design for standard passenger plates. The older standard version with green letters and numbers on white is still in use also. Many people pay an extra fee for license plates that help environmental causes, such as protecting Cape Cod and the Islands or saving the Right Whale.

MICHIGAN

"Great Lakes State"

1914

1966

1998

Michigan started registering vehicles in 1905. Owners received a small numbered disc. They made their own plates out of leather, steel, wood or any other material to display the disc. A standard system using metal plates was in place by 1940. Today's plates feature a "Lake Superior Blue" base with white reflective numbers and letters. A special plate showing the Mackinac Bridge may be purchased for an additional fee.

MINNESOTA

"Land of 10,000 Lakes"

1927

1997

University of Minnesota

Minnesota's standard plate features blue water with a green canoe, green trees with a blue sky, and a winter-white field with a dark blue state shape. The slogan "Explore" appears before the state name at the top. A shortened version of the state nickname, "10,000 Lakes," appears at the bottom. Minnesota also offers specialty plates that help support critical habitats, honor veterans or show pride in one of fourteen colleges.

MISSISSIPPI

"The Magnolia State"

1945

1977

1998

Mississippi State University

Mississippi has created one of the most elegant license plates on the road today. Fancy swirls in the lettering for the state's name touch a white magnolia at the plate's center. The county name appears at the bottom. Passenger vehicle numbers and letters use no special codes; they're unique to each owner. Until 1982, Mississippi used the slogan "The Hospitality State" and it still offers visitors a warm welcome.

MISSOURI

"Show-Me State"

1926

1945

1976

1998

Missouri issued its first state license plates in 1911. It became the first state to use a sticker for showing valid registrations in 1952. Now every state uses stickers, although some require them to be displayed on windshields. Missouri recently changed to a bright plate design. The state name is underlined at the top. A green banner frames the nickname on the bottom. Purple numbers and letters add pizzazz!

MONTANA

"Big Sky Country"

1929

1933

1976

1997

As early as 1933, Montana used the outline of the state on its license plates. This image appears on today's plates, too. Mountain tops underline the state name at the top and the state's nickname, shortened to "Big Sky," accents the bottom. A code in the first two numbers tells the vehicle's home county. The image of a bison skull in the lower right corner reflects the state's Western history.

1933

1940

1976

1999

Nebraska began issuing license plates in 1915. In 1940 and 1941, the state's plates featured an embossed image of the towering state capitol in Lincoln. Today's plates also honor this landmark. The skyline picture shows the famous Chimney Rock, a windmill and city buildings as well. The first two numbers show the vehicle's home county. Nebraskans usually replace their license plates about every three years.

NEVADA

"The Silver State"

1924

1989

1997

Nevada chose many license plate colors from 1916 to 1936. Then it stayed with silver, for its mining heritage, and cobalt blue, the state's official color. Today's plates still use this combination. Nevada last held a complete plate re-issue in 1969, and five plate styles are still valid. The newest design features a silver wilderness scene and cobalt blue Western lettering for the state name.

NEW HAMPSHIRE

"The Granite State"

1918

1999

Antique

New Hampshire plates, first issued in 1905, have been green and white every year except 1978 and 1979. The slogan "Live Free or Die" replaced "Scenic" in 1971. It appears on the top of today's custom plate. Inside a circle on today's standard plate, the "Man in the Mountain" rock outcropping honors one of the state's famous landmarks. Early plates with this design used all numbers.

NEW JERSEY

"Garden State"

1945

1959-79

1991

New Jersey "Pets"

Since 1959, New Jersey has used its state nickname on license plates. "Garden State" remains at the base of the newest design. Today's plates also display the state shape between the first two letters and the four last characters. New Jersey has set aside many letter combinations for special group codes, such as "RI" for Rotary International and "MM" for Merchant Marine. Many specialty plates are also available.

NEW MEXICO

"Land of Enchantment"

1927

1959

1965

1998

New Mexico first issued license plates in 1912. A decorative tab shaped as a diamond, octagon and star showed valid registration on the early porcelain plates. In 1927, New Mexico added the "Zia" Indian sun to its plates. This symbol still appears on today's deep yellow plates. An aqua Indian-style band crosses the top, leaving a space in the center for the county name. Interestingly, New Mexico's plates also say "USA" on them.

NEW YORK

"Empire State"

1920

1976

1986

Notre Dame University

With over ten million registered vehicles today, New York uses three letters and three numbers in many different ways to keep its license plates unique. For example, ABC•123 could be mixed as A12•3BC or AB1•2C3. On standard plates, the Statue of Liberty appears in the center or on the left side. New York also offers several pretty specialty plates, plus captioned plates and letter combinations just for special groups.

1916

1941

1975

1994

The current North Carolina license plate honors the Wright brothers' historic flight at Kitty Hawk. "First in Flight," printed in red, serves as a caption over a blue drawing of the famous airplane. The standard passenger vehicle plate uses three letters and four numbers. Specially issued license plates, such as those for state officials or the disabled, show the same image at the top and a fringe of sea oats at the base.

1949

1962

1976

1996

A park dedicated to peace near the Canadian border inspired the state's nickname. "Peace Garden State" has appeared on license plates since 1956. Today's plate uses the nickname at the bottom and the slogan "Discover the Spirit" at the top. A bright blue sky over a golden prairie earned this design the 1993 "Plate of the Year" Award from serious collectors. The Devil's Lake Sioux and Turtle Mountain Chippewa tribes also issue decorative license plates.

OHIO

"Buckeye State"

1915

1976

1998

Environmental

In 1908, Ohio released its first license plate. The state promoted few slogans over the years, but it currently has two. "The Heart of it All" and "Birthplace of Aviation" began in the 1990s. The state's first system for passenger vehicles used three letters and three numbers separated by the shape of the state. Ohio has added a fourth letter and dropped the state shape to keep up with its growing number of registered vehicles—now over nine million.

OKLAHOMA
"Sooner State"

1945

1997

Environmental

Environmental

The first state-issued license plates in Oklahoma were available in 1915. Since then, the state has used only four slogans. The most recent phrase, "Native America," appears at the bottom of today's plate. Native American symbols separate the green letters and numbers. Vehicle owners may choose colorful personalized plates, scenic conservation plates, or even a "Route 66—Mother Road" plate instead of the standard plate.

OREGON

1935

1974 with '76 tag

1999 "Trail"

1999

Oregon's current license plates show a blue sky, lavender mountains and a green Douglas fir tree between purple letters and numbers. Older issues, still valid, use a yellow sky and a mint-green tree. Oregon vehicle owners may pay a small extra fee for a special plate that honors the Oregon Trail. Fortunately for the state's drivers, Oregon's vehicle registration fees cover a two-year period and rank among the lowest in the nation.

PENNSYLVANIA

"Keystone State"

1912

1997

"Preserve Our Heritage"

"Save Wild Animals"

Pennsylvania uses its official state colors, blue and gold, on its standard license plates. Older plates feature six blue characters on yellow. Newer plates show seven yellow characters on blue. Pennsylvania used its first plate slogan, "Bicentennial State," in 1971. "Keystone State" now appears at the top of plates. This nickname honors the state's history. Pennsylvania held a keystone, or central, position amid the original thirteen colonies.

RHODE ISLAND

"Ocean State"

1926

DISCOVER
ZS·677
RHODE ISLAND. '71

1967 with '71 tab

1983

⚓ •Rhode Island•
PY-264
• Ocean State •

1998

Rhode Island issued its first license plates in 1904. In 1936, the caption "300th Year" honored the state's early history. The word "Discover" appeared on plates from 1967 to 1981. During that time, Rhode Island chose the nickname "Ocean State" for its plates as well. It still appears over a blue wave at the bottom of today's license plates. A small anchor in the upper left corner also serves as a symbol of the state's link to the sea.

SOUTH CAROLINA
"Palmetto State"

1932

1970

1995

2000

The words "Smiling Faces. Beautiful Places" capture the spirit of South Carolina on the most recent standard-issue plates. Blue Appalachian Mountains roll across the plate's top and the state's famous palmetto tree separates the six characters at the center. South Carolina offers many different and colorful designs for special groups, such as veterans and university supporters.

SOUTH DAKOTA
"Coyote State"

1934

1952

1987

1997

Also called the "Home of Mount Rushmore," South Dakota takes great pride in its famous landmark. The granite-carved images of Washington, Jefferson, Lincoln and Theodore Roosevelt also adorn current state plates. The slogan reads, "Great Faces. Great Places." South Dakota codes its license plates by using the numbers to show the vehicle's home county. Three South Dakota Sioux Indian tribes also issue license plates.

TENNESSEE

"Volunteer State"

1937

1959

1997

Environmental

Tennessee issued its first license plates in 1915. Between 1936 and 1956, the plates featured the state shape. License plates issued between 1995 and 2000 honor the state's bicentennial and show an image of the state capitol at the center. Many specialty plates are available with designs for square dancing, the Walking Horse or farming. Beginning in 2000, the slogan "Tennessee Sounds Good to Me" will appear on plates.

TEXAS

"The Lone Star State"

1936

1968

1995

"Space" Plate

Texas license plates have an interesting history which began in 1917. Collectors point to two plates in particular that often confuse people. Texas issued the 1985 Sesquicentennial plate to honor the 150th anniversary of independence from Mexico. The 1995 "150 Years of Statehood" plates honor the date that Texas actually joined the Union. Today's plates show a Texas flag on the right side with a state shape between the characters.

UTAH

"Beehive State"

1945

1986

1998

Utah's location in the Rocky Mountains helped it win the bid for the 2002 Winter Olympics. "Ski Utah!" became its slogan on license plates with the caption, "Greatest Snow On Earth." Vehicle owners may choose the colorful statehood centennial plates or other specialty plates. Utah's "Beehive State" nickname inspired the beehive symbol on the Utah Highway Patrol plates and uniform patches, and on collector plates.

VERMONT

"Green Mountain State"

1945

1967

1997

The state's name comes from a French phrase "vert mont," meaning "green mountain." Vermont uses the translation for its nickname. "Green Mountain State" appears at the base of today's white-on-green license plates. Since 1990, license plates show three letters followed by three numbers. The letters I, J, O, Q, U, V, and Z are not used on these plates to identify Vermont vehicles.

VIRGINIA

"The Old Dominion"

1945

1976

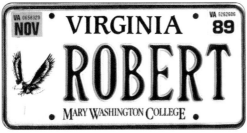
College Plate

"Leaves Plate"

Virginia began registering vehicles in 1906. Today it uses a basic white plate with the state name printed at the top. However, Virginia offers many specialty plates to vehicle owners. These colorfully designed plates, available for an additional fee, have brought the state millions of dollars. One plate shows leaves. Another promotes Virginia Beach. Additional options support wildlife and other special interests.

WASHINGTON

"Evergreen State"

1919

1941

1999

University of Washington

In 1905, Washington registered vehicles for the first time and issued just 763 license numbers. Vehicle owners made their own "plates" from wood, metal or leather, or painted the registrations onto their automobiles. Today, the state registers more than four million vehicles every year. Current plates show Mount Rainier in the background. "Centennial Celebration" appeared on this design from 1987 to 1990, and these plates remain valid.

WEST VIRGINIA

"Mountain State"

1954

1985

1998

Scenic Plate

West Virginia created a new standard-issue plate in 1996 with the slogan "Wild, Wonderful" centered at the bottom. This phrase also appears on plates for the disabled and optional scenic plates. In addition to the scenic plates, special versions for veterans, National Guard members and university fans are available. West Virginia's governor may assign plate numbers 2 -2,000. The number "1" and "ONE" are reserved for the Governor.

WISCONSIN

"Badger State"

1917

1940

1993

1998

Since 1940, Wisconsin license plates have used the "America's Dairyland" slogan. Many people know this phrase better than the official "Badger State" nickname! The current license plate design features a sailboat, geese and a red barn above green and blue lines. Vehicle owners may order specialty plates, including sesquicentennial and environmental designs, for an additional fee. Native American nations within Wisconsin, not the state, issue tribal plates.

WYOMING
"Equality State"

1939

1955

1978

1997

Wyoming license plates have shown a bucking bronco continuously since 1936. Today's design shows the bronco and its rider with mountains in the background. The number to the left of the bronco is coded for the home county. Interestingly, Air National Guard plates use all even numbers; Army National Guard plates use all odd numbers. Wyoming currently offers personalized plates, but no specialty designs.